This edition copyright © 2002 Lion Publishing
Text copyright © 2002 Jean Watson

Published by
Lion Publishing plc
Mayfield House, 256 Banbury Road,
Oxford OX2 7DH, England
www.lion-publishing.co.uk
ISBN 0 7459 4658 5

First edition 2002
10 9 8 7 6 5 4 3 2 1 0

Acknowledgments

15, 19, 27, 30, 36, 45: Job 37:14; James 4:14; Ecclesiastes 3:1; Ecclesiastes
9:10; Mark 6:31; Isaiah 43:19, from the *Holy Bible, New International Version*,
copyright © 1973, 1978, 1984 by International Bible Society. Used by
permission.

Every effort has been made to trace and acknowledge copyright holders of
all the quotations in this book. We apologize for any errors or omissions
that may remain, and would ask those concerned to contact the publishers,
who will ensure that full acknowledgment is made in the future.

A catalogue record for this book is available
from the British Library

Typeset in 12/14 Venetian 301
Printed and bound in China

time

ways to slow down

Jean Watson

Contents

Introduction

• • • • • • • • • • • •

I have been reminding myself of
some astounding facts about time.
Thanks to Einstein and others,
we can no longer think of time as
a constant, but rather as a variable:
at speeds close to that of light,
it actually slows down. Nor is it
separate and independent, but rather
linked to space – hence spacetime;
and this is – incredibly – curved
by planets and stars, rather as a
trampoline curves under the weight
of the person standing or jumping
on it.

Will this amazing arrow end? Leaving the scientists to answer that question in terms of spacetime and the universe, at a personal level we can answer yes in the sense that each human life has a finite length of time on this earth. Meanwhile, what do we do with whatever time we have?

Too busy!

If we are 'too busy', we can miss out on so much that is delightful or important: time with loved ones; time for our inner life; time to develop our gifts and pursue what really fascinates us; time to help others in need; time for play – for walking, enjoying our surroundings, relaxing, being creative; time for unhurried conversations with one another, for laughter and fun, for maintaining friendships…

However, if we are too busy it may not necessarily be because our job demands it and we have no option. Long working hours and constant activity can be a cover for anxiety, a way of not attending to people or issues that we would rather avoid, a distraction from painful emotions, or a proof to ourselves that we are important, significant, popular. It's well worth dealing with these inner agendas – and sooner rather than later.

For, all other considerations aside, the damage from missing out on what's really important may not show up clearly for some time, so we can carry on in the same way assuming that all is well long after it isn't. Sometimes an unwelcome hiccup or interruption can do us a – painful – favour by forcing us to take stock and change.

If you are chafing at some upset to your plans, could you consider whether you are being given an unexpected opportunity to address something you might otherwise have ignored?

What is the point of so much of
our busyness and of our hurry and
our worry and our effort and our
anxiety?

William Barclay

More programmes, more meetings,
more learning experiences, more
relationships, more busyness, until
one becomes so heavy at the surface
of life that the whole person trembles
on the verge of collapse... The
neglected private world can no longer
hold the weight.

Gordon MacDonald

Every day I was absent from my
family is gone for ever.

Billy Graham

Time is a circus always packing up
and moving away.

Ben Hecht

But at my back I always hear
Time's wingèd chariot hurrying near.
And yonder all before us lie
Deserts of vast eternity.

Andrew Marvell

It is flying, irretrievable time is flying.

Virgil

'What would happen if this were not done at all?' If the answer is, 'Nothing would happen,' then obviously the conclusion is to stop doing it. It is amazing how many things busy people are doing that will never be missed!

Peter Drucker

I am sure that no one is indispensable, and that no one should try to be.

William Barclay

Learning to stop is the first step on the road back to sanity.

Edward England

The beauty of work depends upon the way we meet it, whether we arm ourselves each morning to attack it as an enemy that must be vanquished before night comes – or whether we open our eyes with the sunrise to welcome it as an approaching friend who will keep us delightful company and who will make us feel at evening that the day was well worth its fatigue.

Lucy Larcom

Lord, you put twenty-four hours in a day and gave me a body which gets tired and can only do so much. Show me the tasks you want me to do.

Angela Ashwin

Stop and consider God's wonders.

The Bible

Just say no

What else can influence the way we spend our time? One thing may be our inability to say no to other people. Why might this be? Are we wanting to feel needed and important? Afraid of offending the person who is doing the asking, of losing his or her love or approval? Has our upbringing over-emphasized the virtue of pleasing and fitting in with others, or failed to foster a sufficiently strong sense of our own needs and identity?

If any of those are the case, we are making choices on an unsatisfactory basis and our use of time will reflect this. Respecting others and ourselves *equally* sets us free to make unpressurized choices, including those which involve saying no – gently and politely – to others when it would be good and right to do so.

Review what you are currently doing and how you came to be doing those things. Are there any projects or activities which – for

good reasons – you now need to relinquish
in the right way and time? Perhaps such action
would make it possible for you to say yes –
for all the right reasons – to other projects
or activities in the future.

What, of all things in the world,
is the longest and the shortest,
the swiftest and the slowest,
the most divisible and the most
extended, the most neglected
and the most regretted, without
which nothing can be done,
which devours all that is petty
and enlivens all that is great?

Voltaire

Here hath been dawning
Another blue day:
Think, wilt thou let it
Slip useless away?

Thomas Carlyle

Dost thou love life? Then do not
squander time, for that's the stuff
life is made of.

Benjamin Franklin

'Time has too much credit,'
said Bridget. 'I never agree
with the compliment paid
to it. It is not a great healer.
It is an indifferent and
perfunctory one. Sometimes
it does not heal at all. And
sometimes when it seems
to, no healing has been
necessary.'

Ivy Compton-Burnett

What is your life? You are a
mist that appears for a little
while and then vanishes.

The Bible

Most time is wasted not in hours but in minutes. A bucket with a small hole in the bottom gets just as empty as a bucket that is deliberately kicked over.

Paul J. Meyer

Do not walk through time without leaving worthy evidence of your passing.

Pope John XXXIII

Each week brings us 168 golden hours. We spend approximately 56 hours for sleep and recuperation; 28 hours for eating and personal duties; 40–50 hours for earning a living. We have 30–40 hours left to spend just as we wish. But how do we spend them?

Author unknown

In all things, inner silence.

Brother Roger of Taizé

Cultivate freedom of spirit,
spaciousness of mind: live in peace,
boldly and with tranquillity.

Abbé de Tourville

Have peace in your hearts, and
thousands around you will be healed.

St Seraphim of Sarov

Taking stock

• • • • • • • • • • • • •

Some people who are doing valuable and effective work may feel that they aren't. This could be because they're naturally modest. It could also be something they infer from the fact that they are given little or no status or money for what they do. But where would we be without the underrated but immensely important work done by good parents, carers, neighbours, voluntary workers and so on?

A quite different group of people are those who really are less effective than they might be. If we are prepared to reflect on why this might be, things could change for the better. Are we working below par because, if we're honest, we're not really motivated and interested in what we are doing? Or are we tackling something for which we haven't the necessary energy or skills and experience? Or is it just a matter of learning to be more self-disciplined and organized? According to what we discover, we can, if we wish to, start making changes in ourselves or our work, or both.

You might like to do an 'effectiveness rating' on yourself. In the process, you may discover how valid, or otherwise, is the basis on which you are assessing your effectiveness or lack of it!

Anyone can carry his burden,
however hard, until nightfall.
Anyone can do his work,
however hard, for one day.

Robert Louis Stevenson

I long to accomplish a great
and noble task, but it is my
chief duty to accomplish
humble tasks as though they
were great and noble. The
world is moved along, not
only by the mighty shoves
of its heroes, but also by the
aggregate of the tiny pushes
of each honest worker.

Helen Keller

Lost, yesterday, somewhere between
sunrise and sunset, two golden hours,
each set with sixty diamond minutes.
No reward is offered, for they are
gone for ever.

Horace Mann

I made a posy while the day ran by;
Here will I smell my remnant out,
    and tie
My life within this band;
But Time did beckon to the flowers,
    and they
By noon most cunningly did steal away,
And withered in my hand.

George Herbert

Work is love made visible.

Kahlil Gibran

Making a living is best undertaken
as a part of the more important
business of making a life.

Sidney Lovett

The man who wants a garden fair,
Or small or very big,
With flowers growing here and there,
Must bend his back and dig.

Edgar Guest

Every now and then go away,
have a little relaxation, for
when you come back to your
own work your judgment will
be surer; since to remain
constantly at work will cause
you to lose power of judgment.

Leonardo da Vinci

There is a time for everything,
and a season for every activity
under heaven.

The Bible

Work is doing what you now
enjoy for the sake of a future
which you clearly see and desire.
Drudgery is doing under strain
what you don't now enjoy and
for no end that you can
appreciate.

Richard C. Cabot

Disorganized?

• • • • • • • • • • • • •

Some people admit to being disorganized
but manage nonetheless to get through a
tremendous amount of work. Others are
sticklers for order but don't do nearly as much.
I'm a great believer in everyone working in
the way that best suits him or her, but perhaps
those at either end of the spectrum – the
extremely disorganized or the over-organized –
might benefit from moving a little closer to
one another!

People who write or talk about time
management usually suggest that we need,
first of all, to ask ourselves: What is it that
I *really* want to do? Only after that is clear
can we realistically take the next crucial steps
in organizing our time, which are to prioritize
and work out a plan. Much emphasis is placed
on using every spare moment, but some, I was
pleased to note, add that time for family,
friends and fun must not be skimped. I was
also pleased to hear one speaker saying that

interruptions should not *all* be – and
interruptions should *never* be – treated
ruthlessly; if only because of their potential
to be useful or inspiring in some way.

Try making two lists – one of the
important things
in your life and
the other of the
merely urgent ones
– and reflect on
what they might
be telling you.

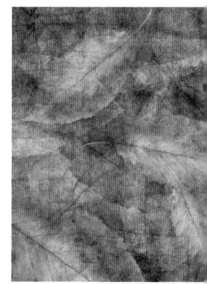

Our greatest danger in life is in permitting the urgent to crowd out the important.

Charles E. Hummel

Procrastination is the thief of time.

Edward Young

I have no Yesterdays,
Time took them away;
Tomorrow may not be –
But I have Today.

Pearl Yeadon McGinnis

Whatever your hand finds to do, do it.

The Bible

You wake up in the morning and lo! your purse is magically filled with twenty-four hours of the unmanufactured tissue of the universe of your life. It is yours. It is the most precious of possessions.

Arnold Bennett

You would do well to budget your time as follows: one half in work, taking care of personal belongings, etc; one fourth in social pastimes with others, both young and old; and one fourth as an interested, pleased observer of life.

William B. Terhune

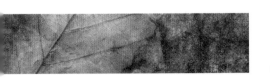

You can be tired *in* the work and not tired *of* the work. It is possible that a man has been over-working and over-taxing his energy and his physical resources. If you go on working too hard or under strain, you are bound to suffer.

Martyn Lloyd-Jones

When you have to make a choice and don't make it, that is in itself a choice.

William James

Nothing puzzles me more than time and space; and yet nothing troubles me less, as I never think about them.

Charles Lamb

Just for today, I will have a quiet half-hour all by myself, and relax. During this half-hour, some time, I will try to get a better perspective on my life.

Kenneth L. Holmes

How completely satisfying to turn from our limitations to a God who has none. For him time does not pass, it remains… God never hurries. There are no deadlines against which he must work. Only to know this is to quiet our spirits and relax our nerves.

A.W. Tozer

Nae man can tether time or tide.

Robert Burns

Time out

We're spoilt for choice – most of us, anyway – when it comes to ways of relaxing and being refreshed. There are dozens of indoor and outdoor sports and pursuits to choose from. Just thinking of people I know gives me a varied list of interests and pastimes. Walking, horse riding, mountain biking, sailing, skiing, painting, pottery; working in silver, growing fuchsias, swimming, exercise classes, cooking, reading, writing poetry, playing video games, visiting museums and galleries, travelling and sightseeing…

So why aren't we all rushing to take time out in one way or another? Maybe money and possessions become such a focus that anything that distracts from acquiring them gets cut out. Or perhaps work has become almost an addiction, giving us status, structure and satisfaction. Possibly it also gives us an excuse not to deal with things we don't want to.

Sadly, if we don't take time out voluntarily, it could well be forced upon us in ways that we would never have chosen.

Try making a list of 'things I would love to do if only I had the time', and then ask of each item: Is there really no way I could make time for this *now*?

● ● ●

Love yourself enough to take a break.

Edward England

The bow cannot always be bent without
fear of breaking.

C.H. Spurgeon

Come with me by yourselves to a quiet place
and get some rest.

The Bible

Something attempted, something done,
has earned a night's repose.

Henry Wadsworth Longfellow

Time, you old gipsy man,
Will you not stay,
Put up your caravan
Just for one day?

Ralph Hodgson

'The time has come,' the Walrus said,
'To talk of many things:
Of shoes — and ships — and sealing wax —
Of cabbages — and kings —
And why the sea is boiling hot —
And whether pigs have wings.'

Lewis Carroll

• • • • • • • • •

Nature never makes haste; her systems revolve at an even pace. The bud swells imperceptibly, without hurry or confusion as though the short spring days were an eternity.

Henry David Thoreau

Time has no divisions to mark its passing. There is never a thunderstorm to announce the beginning of a new month or year.

Thomas Mann

Westerners have watches. Africans have time.

African saying

Time is but a stream I go a-fishing in.

Henry David Thoreau

The Lord is my pacesetter, I shall not rush.
He makes me stop and rest for quiet intervals.
Even though I have a great many things
    to accomplish each day
I will not fret, for his presence is here.
Surely harmony and effectiveness shall be
    the fruit of my hours,
For I shall walk in the pace of my Lord
    and dwell in his house for ever.

Toki Myashina

Time-locked

Someone I knew some years ago was experiencing life as one big anticlimax. He looked back to a time in his career when he felt that he had been at his peak – effective and applauded. But there had been changes since then and in none of the new situations had he been able to recreate the same scenario. He seemed to lose vision, confidence and energy.

There is a kind of weary purposelessness which can set in after a really good or special time. The negative subtext might read: 'I've had my big moment. Nothing else that happens will ever come up to it. From now on it's downhill all the way.' The time of success or contentment, instead of being a continuing source of brightness and joy, starts throwing into shadow everything else in our lives before and after. We begin to lose any sense of expectation and hope.

For quite different reasons we can similarly get stuck and stagnate around our big-but-terrible moments. And yet, however good our highs or however bad our lows, in time we need to learn to see them as episodes in the continuing narrative of our lives – not as the whole story.

If you're stuck and have never tried 'shouting' for help, try it now – or something else that you've never done before!

There are people who are still prisoners
of some adventure in the past.

Paul Tournier

Let us not go over the old ground,
let us rather prepare for what is to come.

Cicero

Look not mournfully into the Past.
It comes not back again. Wisely improve
the Present. It is thine. Go forth to meet
the shadowy Future, without fear.

Henry Wadsworth Longfellow

Time present and time past
Are both perhaps present in time future,
And time future contained in time past.

T.S. Eliot

Time's wheel runs back or stops:
potter and clay endure.

Robert Browning

And time remembered is grief forgotten,
And frosts are slain and flowers begotten,
And in green underwood and cover
Blossom by blossom the spring begins.

Algernon Charles Swinburne

I saw Eternity the other night,
Like a great ring of pure
    and endless light,
All calm, as it was bright;
And round beneath it,
Time in hours, days, years,
Driven by the spheres
Like a vast shadow moved;
    in which the world
And all her train were hurled.

Henry Vaughan

People who dwell in God
dwell in the eternal Now.

Meister Eckhart

'God inhabiteth eternity,'
but eternity stands
with one foot in time.

Frederick Buechner

Lives of great men all remind us
We can make our lives sublime.
And, departing, leave behind us
Footprints on the sands of time.

Henry Wadsworth Longfellow

See, I am doing a new thing! Now it
springs up; do you not perceive it?

The Bible

I think that nothing made is lost;
That not a moon has ever shone,
That not a cloud my eyes hath crossed
But to my soul is gone.
That all the lost years garnered lie
In this the casket, my dim soul:
And thou wilt, once, the key apply,
And show the shining whole.

George Macdonald